THE

DOCTRINE

OF

Imputed Righteousnefs without Works

ASSERTED AND PROVED.

The Works of the LORD *are great, fought out of all them that have Pleasure therein.* Pfalm cxi. 2.

By the late Rev. JOHN GILL, D. D.

PRINTED IN THE YEAR, M DCC.LXXXIV.

THE DOCTRINE

O F

Imputed Righteoufnefs, &c.

ROMANS iv. 6.

Even as David alfo defcribeth the Bleffednefs of the Man unto whom God imputeth Righteoufnefs without Works.

THIS Epiftle is written on purpofe to ftate, ex-
plain, and vindicate, the doctrine of a finner's
juftification before God, by the imputed righteoufnefs of Jefus Chrift In order to which, the Apoftle
takes up his two firft chapters, and part of the third, in
proving, that both Jews and Gentiles are under fin, that
they have by finning broke the law of God, and fo are
become liable to its curfes and condemnation, and therefore cannot be juftified in the fight of God, by their
obedience to it, and then ftrongly and juftly concludes,

B   that

that a man is juftified by faith, in the imputed righteoufnefs of Chrift, without the deeds of the law. This
doctrine he confirms in the beginning of this chapter,
by inftances of two of the greateft men, for religion and
godlinefs, that ever were in the Jewifh nation. The
one is *Abraham*, who was the friend of *God*, and the
father of the faithful, and yet he was not juftified before God by his works; for what faith the Scripture?
Abraham believed God, and it was counted unto him for
righteoufnefs, in ver. 3. The other is *David*, a man after
God's own heart, raifed up by the Lord to fulfill all his
will. Who yet was fo far from trufting to, or depend-
ing upon his own righteoufnefs, for juftification, that he
wholly places the happinefs of men, and fo unqueftion-
ably his own, in a righteoufnefs imputed to him by God,
without works, as in the words I have read unto you.
In fpeaking to which, I fhall,

I. Enquire what that righteoufnefs is, which God im-
    putes to his people for juftification.

II. What is meant by an imputation of it.

III. The manner in which it is imputed to them with-
    out works.

IV. The bleffednefs of thofe perfons, who have it thus
    imputed to them.

I. I fhall inquire what this righteoufnefs is which God
imputes to his people for juftification, and alfo endeavor
to fhew, what it is not, and then what it is.

First; What it is not. And 1. It is not man's obedience to a law of works, because this at best is imperfect, and therefore cannot justify. Those persons who have most eagerly pursued after righteousness by the works of the law, and have made the greatest advances towards it this way, yet have fell abundantly short of it, as the people of *Israel* in general, and in particular the *pharisees*, whose righteousness made the greatest pretences to a justifying one, of any people at the time in which they lived, and yet our Lord says of it, Matt v. 20 *Except your righteousness shall exceed the righteousness of the scribes and pharisees, ye shall in no case enter into the kingdom of heaven.* If it should be said these men were a parcel of hypocrites, and therefore their righteousness is not to be mentioned, with the righteousness of real and sincere Christians, it is easily replied, in the words of the wise man, Eccless. vii. 11. *There is not a just man in the earth, who doeth good and sinneth not.* The most holy men that ever lived on the earth, have been always ready to to acknowlege the imperfections of their obedience and righteousness. Job, was very early convinced of this, and very ingenuous in his confession of it, when he says, Chap. ix. 30, 31. If *I wash myself with snow water and make my hands never so clean, yet shalt thou plunge me in the ditch, and mine own cloaths shall abhor me.* Or, as the words may be rendered, shall cause me to be abhorred; or will discover me to be abominable; that is, my garments of righteousness which I have took so much pains with to work out, make and keep clean, will be so far from rendering me grateful, in the sight of my Judge, that they will rather discover the abominable filthiness of my nature, and so make me the object of his aborrence.

It

It is upon this account, and with the fame view, that *David* defired, *Pfalm* cxliii. 2. *That God would not enter into judgement with him, becaufe that in his fight, no flefh living could be juftified*, that is, by their own righteouf-nefs. And fo the Church in *Ifaiah's* time, Chap. lxiv. 6. acknowledges, that all her *Righteoufnefs were as filthy rags*, and therefore could not be juftifying. Befides this can never be the righteoufnefs intended in my text. Be-caufe this is a righteoufnefs of works. Whereas the righ-teoufnefs God is here faid to impute, is a righteoufnefs without works. Moreover man's obedience to the law of works is his own righteoufnefs. Whereas the righteouf-nefs here mentioned muft be anothers, becaufe it is an im-puted one. A man's own righteoufnefs, inherent in him, needs no imputation of it to him. Add to this, that the bleffednefs of a man, does not confift in, or refult from, his own righteoufnefs, for falvation, which is the whole of a man's happinefs, as to fpiritual things, is not by works of righteoufnefs done by men, but fprings from, and is brought about, by the grace, mercy, and love of God through Chrift; for if man's happinefs confifted in, or was procured by his own righteoufnefs, the grace, mercy, and love of God in man's falvation, would be greatly obfcured and leffened, his wifdom, in the miffion of his Son, would be liable to be impeached and arraigned, his miffion would appear needlefs, as well as his death, as the Apoftle, Gal. ii. 21. argues, *if righteoufnefs comes by the law, then Chrift is dead in vain.* Which argument deferves fpecial notice.

2. This righteoufnefs is not man's obedience to the gofpel as a new and milder law. The fcheme of fome

perfons, if I apprehend it right, is this, that Chrift came
into this world, to relax the old law of works, and to
mitigate and abate the feverities of it, and to introduce
a new law, a gofpel law, a law of milder terms, a re-
med al law, the terms and conditions of which, are
faith, repentance, and fincere obedience, which though
imperfeɛ̃t, is through Chrift and for his fake accepted of,
in the room of a perfeɛ̃t righteoufnefs. The whole of
which fcheme is entirely falfe. For, in the firft place,
Chrift came not into the world, either to deftroy, or
relax the law of God, but to fulfil it, which he did com-
pletly, by his aɛ̃tive and paffive obedience to it. He
fulfilled every jot and tittle of the preceptive part of the
law, which required a holy nature and perfeɛ̃t obedience,
both which were found in him. He bore the whole penalty of the law, in the room and ftead of his people, all
its exaɛ̃tions, requirements and demands were anfwered by
him; all its feverities were executed on him, he was not
fpared or abated any thing, and hereby he magnified the
law, and made it honourable. He indeed freed his people from the curfe and condemnation of it; but has not
either abolifhed or relaxed it, but keeps it in his own
hands as a rule of life and converfation to them, and has
left it in its full mandatory, curfing and damning power
over others without the leaft mitigation, relaxation, or
infringmɛnt of it. Moreover the gofpel is no new law, it
is no law at all, there is nothing in it that looks like a
law, it is called, Aɛ̃ts xx. 24. *The gofpel of the grace of
God*; becaufe it is a difcovery of the exceeding riches of
God s grace in his kindnefs to loft man, through Jefus
Chrift It is called the gofpel of our falvation, becaufe
it reveals the Saviour, it gives an account of his perfon,
office,

office, and grace, and of the great falvation he has wrought out, and points out the perfons who fhall fhare in it, and be everlafting poffeffors of it, as the word ευαγγελιον itfelf tranflated, gofpel, fignifies good news, or glad tidings. Now what is there either in the name, or thing, that looks like a law. The gofpel is no other than a pure promife, a free declaration of peace and pardon, righteoufnefs, life, and falvation to poor finners by Jefus Chrift. The fum and fubftance of it is, *that this is a faithful faying, and worthy of all acceptation, that Jefus Chrift came into the world to fave finners,* 1 Tim. i. 15.

Again; faith and repentance are not the conditions of the new covenant, or terms of any new law, as duties incumbent on us, they belong to the moral law, or law of works, which obliges us to obedience to every thing God does or fhall reveal as his will. As graces beftowed upon us by God, they are parts, they are bleffings of the new covenant of grace, and not conditions of it. Befides, if they were terms or conditions of this new law, or gofpel law talked of, which indeed is a contradiction in terms, they would not be more eafy than the terms of the law of works were to Adam in innocence. Nay it was much more eafy for Adam to have kept the whole law of works, than it is for any of his fallen pofterity to repent and believe of themfelves. And how does this appear to be a remedial law, or a law of milder terms, as it is called.

Once more, it is not confiftent either with the truth or juftice of God, to accept of an imperfect righteoufnefs, though ever fo fincere, in the room of a perfect one. It is not confiftent with his truth, He whofe judgement is

according

according to truth, can never account that a perfect righteousness, which is imperfect. It is not consistent with his justice, he who is the judge of all the earth will do right, and therefore he will by no means clear the guilty, without a full satisfaction to, and a reparation of his broken law. This is the true reason why he set forth Christ to be the propitiation for sin. Namely, that he might appear to be just whilst he was the justifier of him that believes in Jesus. Whereas, was he to justify persons upon the foot of an imperfect Righteousness, he would neither appear just to himself, or to his law, which requires a perfect and complete obedience.

3 This righteousness is not a man's profession of religion, or his submission to the ordinances of the gospel, for men may draw near to God with their mouths, and honour him with their lips, and yet their hearts be removed far from him, and their fear of him be only taught by the precepts of men, they may seek the Lord daily, and seemingly delight to know his ways, as a nation that did righteousness and forsook not the ordinances of their God, they may ask of him the ordinances of justice, and in an outward shew take delight in approaching to him; they may appear to be outwardly righteous before men, and yet be inwardly full of all manner of impurity. May have a name to live and yet be dead, they may have the form of godliness, and yet deny the power thereof; they may submit to the ordinance of baptism, and constantly attend the Lord's supper, and yet be destitute of a justifying righteousness. Yea, even a real and genuine profession of religion, and an hearty submission to gospel ordinances,

from

from right principles to right ends, is not a man's righteoufnefs before God.

4. Neither is fincerity in any religion, no not in the
beft religion, this righteoufnefs, for it is poffible that a
man may be fincerely wrong, as well as fincerely right.
There may be a fincere *Pagan*, or a fincere *Papift*, or a
fincere *Mahometan*, as well as a fincere *Chriftian*. Nay
its poffible for a man to be a fincere *perfecutor* of the true
religion, as well as a fincere *profeffor* of it   The Apoftle
Paul, was fincere in perfecuting the gofpel, as well as
he afterwards was, in preaching that faith he once
deftroyed.   For he thought with himfelf, Acts xxvi. 9.
that he *ought*, in confcience, for the glory of God, and
the advancement of religion, *to do many things contrary to
the name of Jefus of Nazareth*.   And our Lord tells his
difciples, John xvi. 2   that the time was coming,
that whofoever killed them would think that he did God
fervice.   So that fincerity is not a man's righteoufnefs
before God   And indeed take fincerity as a diftinct
grace of the Spirit of God, and it belongs to fanctification, and not to juftification, though it feems rather to
be what runs through every other grace, than to be
diftinct from them ; and is what makes our faith un-
feigned, our love without diffimulation, and our hope
without hypocrify.

5. Nor is the whole real work of grace and fanctification upon the foul its juftifying righteoufnefs, for this
would be to confound juftification and fanctification together ; which two bleffings of grace, though they meet in
one and the fame fubject, and come out of one and the
fame

fame hand, yet are they in themfelves diftinct. Sanctification is a work of grace within us, juftification is an
act of grace upon us. Sanctification is a gradual and
progreffive work; it is fignifie, 2 Pet. iii. 18. by a
growing in grace and in the knowledge of Jefus Chrift;
and it is a work that is but begun, yet is not yet finifhed,
and is carried on by degrees. Juftification is done *fimul
et femel*, it is a compleat act at once, it is expreffed, Col.
ii. 10. by the faints being compleat in Chrift, and per-
fected by his one facri ce.

6. If the whole work of fanctification, is not our
juftifying righteoufnefs before God, then certainly the
to credo c, or act of believeing, which is only a part of
this work, cannot be it. There are indeed fome fcrip-
tures in this chapter wherein is my text, which are by
fome thought to favor this notion, as when it is faid in
ver. 3. *Abraham believed God, and it was imputed to him for
righteoufnefs*, and in ver 5 his faith is counted for righte-
oufi ef, and in ver. 9. for we fay that faith was reckoned
to Abraham for righteoufnefs, in all which places, not the
act of faith, but the object of faith is intended, as will appear from this fingle confideration, namely, that this *it*,
or faith, which was imputed to Abraham, is faid to be imputed to others alfo, as is evident from ver. 22, 23, 24,
and therefore it was imputed unto him for righteoulnefs.
Now if it was not written for h s fake alone, that it was
imputed to him, but for us alfo, to whom *it*, the very felf
fame *it*, fhall be imputed, if we believe on him that raifed up Jefus our Lord from the dead. Now, whatever
reafon perfons may think they have to conclude, that
Abraham's act of faith was imputed to himfelf, as his

C   . juftifying

juſtifying righteouſneſs; yet it cannot with any reaſon be concluded, that his act of faith ſhould be imputed to others alſo as ſuch. The plain meaning is, that object which *Abraham's* faith reſpected and was reckoned to him for his righteouſneſs, is alſo imputed for righteouſneſs to all others who believe in Chriſt. Beſides, it ought to be obſerved, that the apoſtle does not uſe the prepoſition ἀντι but ἰς, he does not ſay that faith was imputed ἀντι δικαιοσυνης inſtead of righteouſneſs, but ἰς ζικαιοσυνην, unto righteouſneſs, and the meaning of the phraſe is the ſame, with the meaning of the words in Rom. x 10. *For with the heart man believeth unto righteouſneſs*, and is expreſſive of the great doctrine of juſtification by faith in the imputed righteouſneſs of Chriſt. That the *to credere*, or act of believing, is not the righteouſneſs intended in my text, may appear yet more manifeſt, from the following con-ſiderations.

1ſt, Faith as a duty performed, or as a grace exerciſed by the believer, is his own, hence we read in ſcripture of my faith, and thy faith, and his faith, the juſt man is ſaid to live by his faith, Heb. xvii. 5. And ſays our Lord to the woman of Canaan, O woman, great is thy faith, be it unto thee even as thou wilt, Matt v 28. And ſays the apoſtle, James ii. 28. ſhew me thy faith without thy works, and I will ſhew thee my faith by my works. But now the righteouſneſs by which a man is juſtified before God, is not his own, but another's, and therefore imputed to him. Hence the Apoſtle Paul deſired to be found in Chriſt, not having on, ſays he, mine own righteouſneſs, which is of the law, Phil. iii 9. Whereas if faith

had

had been his righteoufnefs, he fhould have defired to have on his own righteoufnefs, and not another's.

2d. Faith as fuch is a work of the law, as it is the gift of God, and a grace beftowed upon us, it is a part of the covenant of grace, as has been already obferved, but as it is a duty required of us, and performed by us, it belongs to the law, and is done in obedience to it. It is called the commandment of God. This is his commandment, that ye believe on the name of his Son Jefus Chrift, 1 John iii. 23. It is called the work of God, John vi. 28, 29. not only becaufe it is wrought in us by God, but alfo becaufe it is required of us by him; every command and all duty belongs to the law, as every promife and all grace does to the gofpel. Now if faith, as an act of ours, is our juftifying righteoufnefs, then we are juftified by a work of the law, whereas the fcripture fays, Rom. iii 20. By *the deeds of the law, there fhall no flefh be juftified in his fight.*

3d. Faith is imperfect in the beft of faints; our Lord frequently called his own difciples, men of little faith; and fo confcious were they themfelves of the imperfection of it, that they prayed to him, faying, Luke xvii. 5. Lord increafe our faith. There are τα υςεςηματα της πι ως, fome deficiences, fomething lacking, in the faith of the beft of God's people. Every one has reafon to fay, more or lefs, as the poor man in the gofpel did, Mark ix. 24. *Lord I believe, help thou mine unbelief.* And for this reafon faith cannot be our juftifying righteoufnefs, for that ought to be perfect. Befides, was it perfect, it is but a part of the law. It is indeed one of the weightier matters of the law, as in Matt. xxiii. 23 but then it is not the whole

of

of the law. Now the scripture says, Gal. iii. 10 *Cursed is every one that continueth not in all things, which are written in the book of the law, to do them.* And God whose judgement is according to truth, cannot reckon that a perfect conformity to the law, which is only a partial one.

4th. Faith is manifestly distinguished from righteousness, Rom. x. 10 when a man is said to believe unto righteousness, when the righteousness of God is said to be revealed from faith to faith, and when it is said to be through the faith of Christ, and is called the righteousness of God by faith. Now then, if faith and righteousness are two different things, then faith is not our justifying righteousness, and so not the righteousness mentioned in my text.

5th. Something else is represented, as the righteousness by which a sinner is justified before God. The people of God, are said to be justified freely by the grace of God, through the redemption that is in Christ Jesus, and some times by the blood of Christ, and at other times by the one man's obedience, Rom. ii. 24 and vi 9—19. Now, faith is not the redemption in Christ Jesus, nor is it the blood of Christ, nor is it his obedience either active or passive, and therefore is not that which is imputed for justification

Nevertheless, faith must be allowed to have a very great concern in the business of justification. Hence we are said to be justified by faith, Rom. v. 1. not by faith either as a work performed by us, or as a grace wrought in us, but we are justified by it relatively or objectively, as it respects, apprehends, and lays hold on Christ and his

righteousness

righteousnefs for juftification; or we are juftified by it organically, as it is a recipient of this blefling, for faith is the hand which receives the blefling from the Lord, and righteoufnefs from the God of our falvation. Faith is that grace to which this righteoufnefs is revealed, and by which the foul firft fpies it. When beholding its glory, fufficiency and fuitablenefs, it approves of it, and renounces its own righteoufnefs. It is that grace by which a foul puts on Chrift's righteoufnefs as its garment, and rejoices therein, by which all boafting in a man's own works is excluded, and by which all the glory of juftification is given to Chrift. But I proceed,

Secondly, To fhew, what is this righteoufnefs intended in my text, which God imputes unto his people, and that is, the righteoufnefs of our Lord Jefus Chrift. By which I mean not his effential righteoufnefs as God, as *Ofiander* dreamed For though he who is our Righteoufnefs is *Jehovah*, Jerem. xxiii. 6 yet that righteoufnefs of his by which he is *Jehovah*, is not our juftifying righteoufnefs, but that which refults from his active and paflive obedience as Mediator, Rom v. 1. For by one man's obedience many are made righteous, or is, that righteoufnefs of Chrift, which confifts of the holinefs of his nature, the conformity of his life and actions to the law of God, and his fuftaining the whole penalty of that law, in the room and ftead of his people. In the commendation of which righteoufnefs, many things might be faid; let thefe few following fuffice at prefent.

1. It is a law honouring, and a juftice fatisfying righteoufnefs, and therefore God is well pleafed with it, Rom.

v. 9.

v. 9. is well pleafed for his righteoufnefs fake, becaufe he hath magnified the law and made it honourable   The law is made more honourable by Chrift's obedience to it, than it is by the obedience of all the angels in heaven, or than it could be by all God's people on earth, fuppofing their obedience was never fo perfect.   The reafon is becaufe of the greatnefs of his perfon, he being God as well as man, who obeyed and wrought out a righteoufnefs, which is alfo fuch an one, as juftice can find no fault with, but is entirely fatisfied with, and in which God's people appear even in the eye of juftice, unblameable, and irreproveable --- 2. It is perfect and compleat, and acquits from all fin and condemnation, thofe who are interefted it in, are perfectly comely thro' the comelinefs which is put upon them , they are compleat in Chrift, the head of all principality and power; they are juftified by this righteoufnefs, from all things, from which they could not be juftified by the law of *Mofes* , they are freed from all guilt of fin, are not under obligation to punifhment, and fhall not enter into condemnation ; their fins are now covered and hid, from the eye of divine juftice, and when they are fought for hereafter fhall not be found.

3. It is the righteoufnefs of God, and fo ferves for many ; if it had been only by the righteoufnefs of a creature, it could have been of no ufe and fervice, but to the creature who was the author of it , but it being the righteoufnefs of God, it is to all and upon all that believe , many are made righteous by it, even all the elect of God and feed of Chrift   For in him fhall all the feed of Ifrael be juftified and fhall glory. It is a garment down to the foot, and
                                                                    covers

covers every member, even the meaneſt and loweſt in Chriſt's myſtical body.

4. It is an everlaſting righteouſneſs. Our righteouſneſs is both imperfect and of a ſhort continuance. Like *Ephraim's* goodneſs, it is as the morning cloud and the early dew. But Chriſt's righteouſneſs will abide for ever, it is a garment that will never wear out, or wax old, it is a righteouſneſs that will laſt our lives, be of ſervice at death, appear freſh at judgement, and will anſwer for us in a time to come, and give us an abundant entrance into the everlaſting kingdom of our Lord Jeſus Chriſt.

5. It is a better righteouſneſs than *Adam* had in innocence, or the angels now have in heaven. *Adam's* righteouſneſs was the righteouſneſs of a creature, but this the righteouſneſs of God. That was looſeable and was actually loſt, Eccleſ. vii. 9, for God made man upright, but he ſought out many inventions, in ſeeking which he loſt his righteouſneſs; but Chriſt's righteouſneſs can never be loſt, it abides for ever. The ſame may be ſaid of the righteouſneſs of Angels, which at beſt is but a creature righteouſneſs, and might be loſt, as it was by a large number of them, and might have been by the reſt, had it not been for confirming grace from Chriſt. Chriſt's righteouſneſs may well be called, Luke xv 22. the beſt robe, for it is ſuch an one as *Adam* never had to his back in innocence, or the angels now have in glory. But I go on,

II. To enquire what is meant by the imputation of this righteouſneſs, which is the way in which it becomes

ours,

ours and indeed is the only way in which it can become ours. The Hebrew word חשב ufe in Gen xv. 6. and the greek word λογιζομαι ufed by the apoftle here, fignifies to eftimate, reckon, impute, or place fomething to the account of another. So the righteoufnefs of Chrift is eftimated, reckoned, and imputed to be his people's, and is placed to their account as fuch by God the Father, and looked upon as much by him as their juftifying righteoufnefs, or as though it had been wrought by them, in their own perfons. That this righteoufnefs becomes ours this way, is manifeft. For in the fame way that Adam's fin became ours, the fame way the righteoufnefs of Chrift becomes ours ; or the fame way we are made finners by the difobedience of Adam, are we made righteous by the obedience of Chrift. Rom. v. 19. *For as by one man's difobedience, many were made finners. So by the obedience of one, fhall many be made righteous.* Now Adam's fin became ours, or we were made finners, through his fin, by imputation, it was reckoned, it was placed to the account of all his pofterity. So Chrift's righteoufnefs becomes ours, or we are made righteous, through that righteoufnefs of his, by the imputation of it to us, it is reckoned, it is placed to our account. Again, the fame way our fins became Chrift's, Chrift's righteoufnefs becomes ours, as appears from Cor. v. 21. He who knew no fin, was made fin for us, that we might be made the righteoufnefs of God in him. Now the way in which Chrift was made fin for us, was by imputation, he never had any fin inherent in him, though he had it transferred unto him and laid upon him So the way in which we are made the righteoufnefs of God, muft be by the imputation of Chrift's righteoufnefs, and

indeed

indeed we cannot be made righteous any other way, than by imputation. For the objects of juſtification are ungodly perſons in themſelves, for God juſtifies the ungodly, as in the verſe preceding my text. Now if they are ungodly in themſelves, then they are not juſtified by a righteouſneſs of their own, it muſt be by the righteouſneſs of another.' And if they are juſtified by the righteouſneſs of another, that other's righteouſneſs, muſt be ſome way or other made their's, it muſt be placed to their account, and reckoned as their own, which is only done by an imputation of it to them. But,

III. I ſhall now conſider the manner in which this righteouſneſs is thus imputed, and that is, without works. That this righteouſneſs is imputed without works, is manifeſt from the character the perſons bear, whom God juſtifies, which is that of ungodly ones, as has been juſt now obſerved. If they are ungodly, they are without works; good works, or works of righteouſneſs. It God therefore will juſtify ſuch, as he certainly does, he muſt juſtify them by imputing a righteouſneſs to them, without any conſideration of works done by them. And, indeed, if God did not impute righteouſneſs for juſtification in this manner, juſtification would not be an act of free grace, as it is always repreſented to be. We may argue about juſtification, as the Apoſtle does about election, when he ſays, Rom. xi. 6. and if of grace, then it is no more of works, otherwiſe grace is no more grace. But if it be of works, then it is no more grace, otherwiſe work is no more work. We are ſaid, Titus iii. 7. to be juſtified, not only by the grace of God, but freely by his grace, to expreſs the abundance and freeneſs of divine grace, in the

D   free

free gift of righteoufnefs unto juftification of life. Befides, if righteoufnefs was not imputed without works,
boafting would not be excluded, as it is in God's way of
juftifying finners, by Chrift's righteoufnefs, without any
confideration of them. And, indeed, works are not caufes
of any fort in the affair of juftification, they are not the
moving caufe of it . For that is the free grace of God ;
nor are they the material caufe of it, for that is the obedience and righteoufnefs of Chrift. Nor are they the in-
ftrumental caufe, for that is faith, nor are they the *caufa a*
fine qua non, or caufes without which perfons are juftified,
who never performed good works. And indeed thofe
that are juftified, are juftified, if not without the prefence
of them, yet without the efficiency of them, or any confideration of them as having any cafual influence on juftification, for with reference hereunto, they are not to be
admitted into the loweft clafs or range of caufes. It may
perhaps be faid, how then can the Apoftles, *Paul* and *James*,
be reconciled in this matter, feeing the one pofitively
affirms, Rom iii. 28. that a man is juftified by faith,
without the works of the law; and the other, James ii.
21. 24, 25. as pofitively afferts, that a man is juftified,
by works, and not by faith only. To which I anfwer,
there are two things, which when obferved, will rectify
and quickly remove the feeming difficulty, and reconcile
the Apoftles to each other, which are, 1. They fpeak
of two different things. The Apoftle *Paul* fpeaks of the
juftification of a man's perfon before God, and this he
truly afferts to be, by a righteoufnefs imputed without
works. The Apoftle *James* fpeaks of a juftification of
a man's faith, or of his caufe before men, which he alfo
truly afferts to be by works, for wifdom is juftified of her
children,

children, Matt. xi. 19. True and undefiled religion is dif-
covered and bore witness to by good works. Faith is shewn
forth, made known, and evidentially perfected by them|;
in justificati n by imputed righteousness, a man has not
whereof to boast before God. In justification of a man's
cause by works, a man has whereof to boast before men,
and in some cases with a becoming modesty may say with
Samuel, 1 Sam. xii. 3. Whose ox have I taken ? whose
ass have I taken ? or whom have I defrauded ?

2. They speak to two different sort of persons. The
Apostle *Paul* had to do with self *Justiciaries*, who sought
for righteousness not by faith, but as it were by the works
of the law, who being ignorant of God's righteousness,
went about to establish their own righteousness, and so sub-
mitted not to the righteousness of Christ. The Apostle
James had to do with a set of men called *Gnosticks*, who
boasted of their knowledge, from whence they took their
name. These were the *Libertines and Antinomians* of that
day, who trusting to their speculative notions and histo-
rical faith, despised the law, and disregarded and neg-
lected the performance of good works, accounting
their knowledge sufficient unto salvation. And this also
occasioned those different modes of expression in these
Apostles, who otherwise were agreed in the same truths.
I go on,

IV. To consider the blessedness of those persons
who have this righteousness imputed to them. 1. They
are freed from all sin and condemnation, not from the
being of sin, but from the guilt of it, and all obligation
to punishment. Rom. viii. 1. For there is no condemnation

demnation to them who are in Chiift Jefus, to them
who are made the righteoufnefs of God, in him, they
may fay as the Apoftle did, Rom. viii. 33, 34. Who
fhall lay any thing to the charge of God's elect? it is
God that juftifies, who fhall condemn; it is Chrift that
died. And therefore they muft be happy perfons, for
bleffed is the man whofe iniquities are forgiven, and
whofe fin is covered, bleffed is the man to whom the
Lord will not impute fin, with which words David,
Pfalm xxxii. 1. defcribeth the bleffednefs of the
perfons interefted in this righteoufnefs.---2. Their perfons and fervices are both acceptable to God, he is well
pleafed with both, for Chrift's righteoufnefs fake.
Chrift's garments fmell of myrrh, aloes and caffia, with
which his people being clad, the Lord fmells a fweet
fmell in them, as the fmell of a field which the Lord hath
bleffed; their perfons come up with acceptance before
him, and their facrifices both of prayer and praife are
grateful to him, through the perfon, blood, righteoufnefs
and mediation of Chrift's righteoufnefs which is imputed to them, fhall never be taken away from tnem, is one
of thofe bleffings he will never reverfe, and one of thofe
gifts of his which are without repentance.—4 It fhall
go well with thefe perfons in life, at death, and at judg-
ment, Ifaiah iii. 10. *Say ye to the Righteous it fhall go well
with him.* It fhall go well with him in life, for all things
work together for his good. It fhall go well with him
at death. For the righteous hath hope in his death,
founded upon this righteoufnefs imputed to him. It
fhall go well with him at judgnent, for this righteoufnefs
will anfwer for him at that time, and bring him off clear
at God's bar, and introduce him into his kingdom and
glory.

glory.——5. Such perfons are heirs of glory, and fhall everlaftingly enjoy it, for being juftified by grace, they are made heirs according to the hope of eternal life. Juftification and glorification are clofely connected together. For whom God juftified, them he alfo glorified, Rom. viii. 30. Juftified perfons may comfortably argue, from their juftification, to their glorification, and ftrongly conclude with the apoftle, Rom. v. 9. That if they are juftified by the blood of Chrift, they fhall be faved from wrath through him. I fhall add no more, but fome fhort improvement of what has been faid, and

1. Seek firft the kingdom of God and his righteoufnefs, for without a righteoufnefs there will be no admittance into heaven, and fuch an one it muft be, as is commenfurate to all the demands of God's righteous law, for no other will be fatisfactory to divine juftice.—2. Go to Chrift for fuch an one, in whom only it is to be had, who is the end of the law for righteoufnefs, to every one that believes, Rom. x. 4. it may be had in him, it cannot be had in any other. For furely, or only, fhall one fay, in the Lord have I righteoufnefs and ftrength, Ifaiah xlv. 24.

3. Admire the grace of God, in imputing this righteoufnefs to you, and rejoice therein, it is grace in Chrift to procure, and grace in the Father to impute it, and grace in the Spirit to apply it. Admire the grace of each perfon herein, and afcribe the glory of your juftification to it.

4. Miferable will thofe perfons be, who will be found at the laft day without this righteoufnefs, for fuch fhall

E

not

not inherit the kingdom of God, they will not be admit-
ed into the wedding chamber, not having on the wedding
garment, but orders will be given to bind them hand
and feet, and caſt them into outer darkneſs, where will
be weeping, wailing and gnaſhing of teeth.

☞ This Sermon was never before Printed.

F I N I S;

4 OC 58